Lifesize
Rainforest

Written by Anita Ganeri
Illustrated by
Stuart Jackson-Carter

KINGFISHER
NEW YORK

KINGFISHER
LONDON & NEW YORK

Copyright © Kingfisher 2014
Published in the United States by Kingfisher
175 Fifth Ave., New York, NY 10010
Kingfisher is an imprint of
Macmillan Children's Books, London.

Consultant: Michael Bright
Editor: Clare Hibbert
In-house editor: Carly Madden
Design and styling: Maj Jackson-Carter
Cover design: Mike Davis

Distributed in the U.S. and Canada
by Macmillan, 175 Fifth Ave.,
New York, NY 10010

Library of Congress Cataloging-in-Publication data
has been applied for.

ISBN: 978-0-7534-7190-6 (HB)
ISBN: 978-0-7534-7191-3 (PB)

Kingfisher books are available for special promotions and premiums. For details contact:
Special Markets Department, Macmillan, 175 Fifth Ave., New York, NY 10010.

For more information, please visit www.kingfisherbooks.com

Printed in China
1 3 5 7 9 8 6 4 2
1TR/0714/WKT/UG/128MA

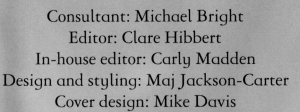

Contents

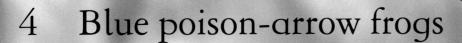

How many female frogs can you spot? Turn to page 32 to check.

4

Blue poison-arrow frogs

As a male poison-arrow frog sits and calls, a group of females gathers. Two of them even start to fight! Just one will become his mate. After mating, both parents guard the eggs until they hatch. Then they carry the tadpoles to tiny treetop ponds, formed from water caught in bromeliad flowers.

Bee hummingbirds

A pair of the world's tiniest birds flits around a hummingbird bush. Using their long, pointed beaks, they reach deep inside the scarlet flowers to drink the sweet nectar. In order to feed, bee hummingbirds hover in one place and beat their wings in a figure-eight pattern 80 times per second—so fast that they look like a blur.

Goliath beetles

Handsome Goliath beetles battle on a tree branch.
These two are males, fighting over territory or to win a
female's attention. Gripping on tightly with their sharp
claws, the beetles push at each other with their Y-shaped
horns, until the unlucky loser tumbles off the tree.

Philippine tarsiers

In the rainforest, night is falling. A baby
Philippine tarsier clings onto its mother's back
as she hunts for insects to eat. After locating her
prey with her enormous eyes, she will catch it in
her hands. Her long, slender fingers form a cage
to stop the flapping insect from getting away.

11

Queen Alexandra's birdwing butterflies

A pair of Queen Alexandra's birdwing butterflies flies high up above the rainforest canopy. It is easy to tell the male and the female apart—the male is smaller and more colorful. The biggest butterflies in the world, these magnificent insects began life as tiny eggs laid on poisonous pipe vine leaves.

Raggiana bird of paradise

During the breeding season, a male Raggiana bird of paradise puts on a spectacular show. He takes up his perch on the branch of a tree. Then he lowers his head, claps his wings, shrieks loudly, and puffs out his gorgeous tail feathers. This display is aimed at attracting a female—she chooses the showiest male.

Parson's chameleon

Standing perfectly still on a tree branch, a Parson's chameleon grips on tightly with its mittenlike feet. Only its big, bulging eyes show any signs of movement, swiveling around in search of insects to eat. When the chameleon spots one, it shoots out its long, sticky tongue and snaps up the prey, with lightning speed.

Golden-crowned flying fox

A golden-crowned flying fox, one of the world's biggest bats, spends the day roosting upside-down on a branch. It shares its tree with other flying foxes for protection from its enemies. When night falls, the bat flies many miles through the forest searching for juicy figs—its favorite food.

Mandrill

With a face of red and blue and a bright bottom to match, a male mandrill is a magnificent sight. Striking markings attract females, but they also make it easier for the monkeys to follow each other through the thick forest. Mandrills live in large family groups called troops—the male with the boldest colors becomes the troop leader.

Jaguar

As evening falls in the rainforest, a solitary jaguar sets out to hunt for food. This beautiful beast has a powerful, muscular body and jaws strong enough to bite through a turtle's shell. A superb swimmer and climber, the jaguar lies in wait for prey and, then leaps out when a victim comes close.

Malayan tapir

Shuffling slowly through the undergrowth, a Malayan tapir makes frequent stops to munch on twigs, leaves, and fruit. It guides the food into its mouth with its long, fleshy snout. The tapir is mostly out at night, using the same well-worn paths through the forest to find the best places to feed.

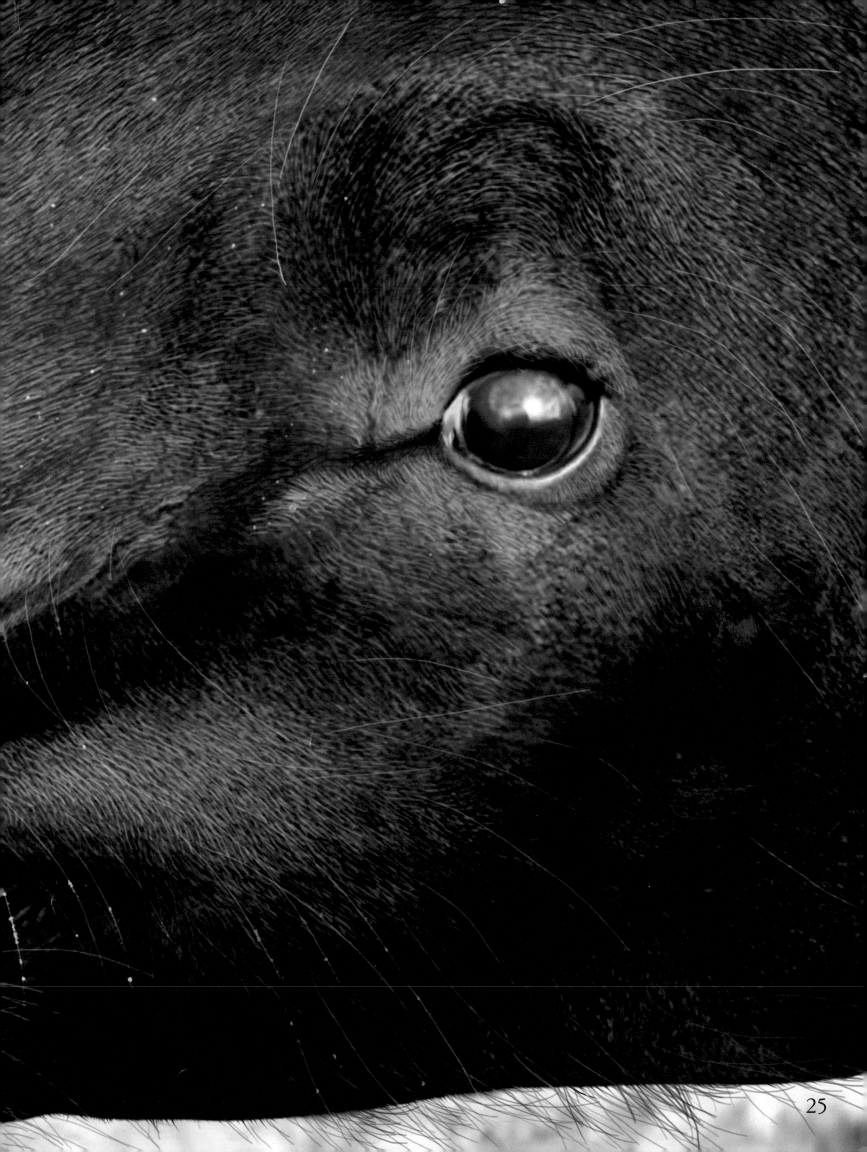

Green anaconda

A green anaconda lurks in the river. Having eyes and nostrils on top of its head means that it can still see and breathe. The snake waits for a tapir or other animal to come down to the water's edge, grabs it, coils around it, and squeezes it to death. Then the anaconda swallows its meal whole.

Animal facts

Each frog has its own unique pattern of black spots.

Bee hummingbirds lay eggs the size of peas in tiny, cup-shaped nests.

These butterflies sip flower nectar using their long, strawlike tongues.

UNDER THREAT

UNDER THREAT

UNDER THREAT

Blue poison-arrow frog

Rainforest habitat: Suriname and Brazil, South America

Length: 1.2–1.8 in. (3–4.5cm)

Weight: Around 0.3 oz. (8g)

Diet: Mostly insects

Average lifespan: 4–6 years

Amazing fact: The blue poison-arrow frog's eye-catching colors are not simply for show. They warn other animals that the frog is deadly poisonous to eat.

Bee hummingbird

Rainforest habitat: Cuba, Central America

Length: Around 2.2 in. (5.5cm)

Weight: Up to 0.07 oz. (1.9g)

Diet: Nectar and small insects

Average lifespan: Up to 7 years

Amazing fact: To keep up their energy, bee hummingbirds have to eat half of their weight in food each day and drink up to eight times their weight in water.

Queen Alexandra's birdwing butterfly

Rainforest habitat: Papua New Guinea, Oceania

Length: 3 in. (8cm) (female); 2.4 in. (6cm) (male)

Wingspan: 12 in. (30cm) (female); 7.5 in. (19cm) (male)

Weight: Around 0.4 oz. (12g) (female); around 0.3 oz. (9g) (male)

Diet: Nectar

Average lifespan: 3 months (adult)

Amazing fact: Queen Alexandra's birdwing butterfly was discovered in 1906. It was named as a compliment to the British queen at that time, Alexandra, wife of King Edward VII.

Females lay their eggs in the soil. They dig holes with their heads.

Tarsiers have pads on their fingers and toes to help them grip.

Goliath beetle

Rainforest habitat: Africa

Length: Up to 4 in. (11cm) (male); up to 3 in. (8cm) (female)

Weight: Around 1.8 oz. (50g)

Diet: Tree sap and fruit

Average lifespan: Less than 1 year

Amazing fact: Goliath beetles are some of the biggest insects in the world. Male beetles can grow as big as your hand and weigh as much as three mice.

Philippine tarsier

Rainforest habitat: Philippines, Southeast Asia

Length of head and body: Up to 6 in. (16cm)

Length of tail: Up to 10.8 in. (27.5cm)

Weight: Up to 6 oz. (165g)

Diet: Mostly insects, especially crickets and grasshoppers

Average lifespan: 10 years (in captivity)

Amazing fact: A Philippine tarsier cannot swivel its eyes in their sockets but can turn its head almost all of the way around to look out for prey.

UNDER THREAT

UNDER THREAT

UNDER THREAT Animals are under threat if their numbers are falling and they risk becoming extinct (dying out forever). Or they may be under threat because their habitat is disappearing.

A chameleon's tongue is more than twice as long as its body.

Birds of paradise are related to crows and starlings.

Parson's chameleon

Rainforest habitat: Madagascar

Length: Up to 27.6 in. (70cm)

Weight: Around 25 oz. (700g)

Diet: Insects, lizards, and birds

Average lifespan: More than 6 years

Amazing fact: A Parson's chameleon can change the color of its skin to blend in with its surroundings, communicate with other chameleons, or regulate its body temperature.

The golden-crowned flying fox gets its name from its crown of golden hairs.

Raggiana bird of paradise

Rainforest habitat: Papua New Guinea, Oceania

Length: Around 13 in. (34cm)

Wingspan: Up to 25 in. (63cm)

Weight: Around 9.5 oz. (270g) (male); around 6.2 oz. (175g) (female)

Diet: Fruit, berries, and insects

Average lifespan: Unknown, but other birds of paradise live for more than 30 years in captivity

Amazing fact: Groups of up to 10 Raggiana birds of paradise gather in one tree. The same tree may have been used by many generations of birds.

Golden-crowned flying fox

Rainforest habitat: Philippines, Southeast Asia

Length: Up to 12 in. (31cm)

Wingspan: Up to 5.6 ft. (1.7m)

Weight: Around 2.6 lb. (1.2kg)

Diet: Fruit, mostly figs

Average lifespan: 15 years

Amazing fact: A young flying fox will cling to its mother's fur with its claws. She fans it with one of her wings to keep it cool.

Mandrill

Rainforest habitat: West Africa

Length: Up to 35 in. (90cm)

Weight: Up to 77 lb. (35kg)

Diet: Fruit (50%); seeds, leaves, and flowers (45%); insects, spiders, amphibians, eggs, birds, and small mammals (5%)

Average lifespan: 20 years

Amazing fact: Mandrills have huge canine teeth, more than 2 in. (5cm) long. They look scary when they shake their heads and bare their teeth, but actually, they are being friendly.

UNDER THREAT

Mandrills store food in large pouches in their cheeks to eat later.

Jaguars sometimes kill prey by piercing its skull with their sharp teeth and biting into the brain.

Jaguar

Rainforest habitat: Central, South, and southwestern North America

Length of head and body: Up to 6 ft. (1.85m)

Length of tail: Up to 36 in. (91cm)

Weight: Up to 249 lb. (113kg)

Diet: Mammals, reptiles, and fish

Average lifespan: 12–15 years

Amazing fact: Most jaguars have tawny-orange fur with black rosette-shaped markings. But some have such dark coats that you can barely see their spots.

UNDER THREAT